The Shepherd's Tent

How to Embrace Rest in God Amid a Chaotic World

Mark Casto

Mark Casto has a voice for his generation and beyond, and it is a voice of wisdom and maturity. This message is for everyone, regardless of physical age or "ministry age." Come apart before you come apart. I have great respect for Mark and his obedience to truly know Christ and walk with Him, without regard for the opinion or approval of man. Dive into this book and be awakened to the relationship our Father truly desires with each one of us, and I believe your eyes and ears will be opened to His love and destiny for you.

Tim Sheets, Apostle, Author of *Angel Armies*, *Planting the Heavens*, and *New Era of Glory*

There are books that are meant to inform, and there are books that provoke you to transform. *The Shepherd's Tent* does both. Mark invites you into his journey as he transitions from the busyness of performance into a world where Abba's care transforms your very innermost desires. This is not a "how to" kind of book, but it's an invitation to show you the path to unveil the authentic you. If this book speaks to anything, it's that Abba's care for you is absolute. He wants nothing more than a genuine connection with you that has nothing to do with "how well" you're doing, but reveals His heart for you. The Lemleys are honored not only to call the Castos our friends, but also to call them our family. We are witnesses of the joy that they have discovered on this path. We are confident that what Mark shares about their journey can be a lamp shining for you as you find yourself leaving the chaos of Babylon for the care you will find in the Shepherd's tent.

Bobby Lemley, Prophet, Founder of City on A Hill in Charleston, SC

Simply put, you need to read this book. Especially those of us who grew up in the religious system that demanded rushing, forced striving, and perpetuated anxiety all in the name of "serving God." Mark has a unique ability to write in such a deep, yet understandable, way that connects with the reader and fills us with the hope of a more excellent way. This book is raw; it's vulnerable and honest, and will be an important piece in calling a generation back to the Shepherd's tent. His intention for us all is rest, and this book stands as a lighthouse from Babylon's never-ending wheel of performance. Read it, read it again, and let Mark's journey be a testimony to your spirit that rest is truly your inheritance.

Matt Brown, Pastor of The Homestead in Aubrey, TX

The Shepherd's Tent by Mark Casto is a precious gift to the body of Christ. As you read it, you will be challenged to acknowledge the often-frantic pace culture has set before you, and will be given the tools to reframe your life in light of the revelation of the Father's love. [This book] is prophetic, personal, and practical, and will be a fresh wind in the sails of any leader. It is my honor to lend my voice of endorsement and commendation to this wonderful book by my good friend.

Mattie Montgomery, The Altar Fellowship, Johnson City, TN

In Hebrews 4, the writer tells us to strive for one specific thing: rest. An interesting pairing, I think—strive and rest? It almost seems oxymoronic. Maybe it's better understood this way: if there's one thing worth using your effort to attain, use it to pursue the rest God has already provided for you. God has a place of rest for us. It is real and available. What a beautiful reality.

In this book, my good friend Mark Casto takes us on a journey of his "entering into rest." His road to enter this "faith-rest life." I was an eyewitness to the beautiful process God worked in him to ultimately find and enter into the rest of God. As a friend, I'm so thankful he found this place. As a fellow minister to God's people, I'm so thankful the Lord has commissioned him to share his story and the glorious truths he found along the way.

May this book be a launching pad for you. May it gloriously lead you into the Father's care and rest. I believe it will.

Bryn A. Waddell, Pastor, City Revival Church in Kannapolis, NC

The earth is groaning for a manifestation of the sons and daughters of God. Although in many circles, "church" has become a principle-driven operation focused on optical metrics, there is an organic movement of authentic and undomesticated Kingdom people whose hearts burn for the original intent of the Father. In *The Shepherd's Tent*, Mark Casto powerfully articulates the heart and the essence of this tribe who have been indelibly branded by the blaze of belovedness.

Bishop Kevin Wallace, Redemption To The Nations Church in Chattanooga, TN

To my four children: Elijah, Ezekiel, Elliana, and Eden. By the grace of God, I was given permission to slow down so I could watch you grow. You get more glorious with each day. I love you!

—Dad

CONTENTS

A Divine Romance

It was a Saturday night, 11:30 p.m. My heart began to race, my chest tightened, and a subtle voice whispered, *"They will find you dead in this room tomorrow."* Not quite the way I'd imagined the afterglow of a glorious service that night.

The next week, I was in a cardiologist's office at the age of twenty-five, only to discover that my heart issue was much deeper than the physical organ: I was dealing with anxiety.

Anxiety from what? I was living the ministry dream. I was married with three kids. I was traveling the nation, preaching, and our ministry at home had exploded from six people to hundreds weekly, with thousands attending our conferences. This was prophecy fulfilled, dreams coming true. Another West Virginia boy had escaped the mountains of obscurity to change the world. Yet amid the greatest days of ministerial success, my interior world was falling apart.

I had stopped flying because of fear, so I drove to every preaching engagement. I could not travel alone, because if left to silence, my mind tormented me. My sleep was at a minimum, and each morning began with a sore jaw from clenching my teeth. Self-diagnosing myself with any feeling that seemed abnormal in my body, I constantly braced for the worst.

How could this be happening to me? I was a "prophetic evangelist," a pastor, a "man of God." Was this warfare? Maybe a thorn in my flesh? But I discovered this was worse than a demon: it was me. I was addicted to the ministry, enslaved to the applause of man, and I could not escape the treadmill of performance. This was the sad result of being thrust into the ministry at eighteen years old because of noticeable gifts instead of being established in the gospel and rooted in Abba's love.

I knew something needed to change, but I had no framework for a more excellent way. Onward, Christian soldier! There I sat, looking to other leaders and heroes, only to discover that these men were reaching the world yet losing the spark in their marriages and their connections with their children. Was this the gospel—sacrificing family on the altar of fulfilling personal destiny?

In the eyes of many, I was living the dream. Thousands would run to the altar, tears running down their faces, with reports of healing and deliverance everywhere we went. Yet I was numb. My devotion was no longer about intimacy because the pressure to bring something fresh to God's people (sometimes six times a week on the road and at home) was now my responsibility. This dream of full-time ministry was becoming a nightmare.

How could I break this cycle? Preaching weekly, office hours, pastoral duties, and the life of the evangelist at least forty-two weekends a year. Those weekends included multiple services and meetings as well as time spent with other leaders. The ministry was outgrowing me. Finally, when I was hosting our biggest conference of the year, the voice of the Lord interrupted my message. I was trying to preach while the Lord was talking to me. He said, "The spirit of 1776 has come upon this generation. Just as your forefathers cast off the yoke of the tyranny of Great Britain, so shall this generation cast off the yoke of the tyranny of religion and come into the glorious liberty of being the sons and daughters of Yahweh. And if you want to be a part of it, you will be required to make revolutionary decisions."

That one moment with Abba led me to the most revolutionary decision of my life. I had to admit that *I* was the one yoked to religion. I had to admit that my pace was off from the way of Jesus. I had to have enough humility to admit that I had traded intimacy with Jesus for ministry to people. Because of a faulty religious system, we applauded growth in ministry over personal growth in devotion.

To the surprise of many, I resigned from the ministry I had helped to birth. I didn't know what exactly was next, but I could not let this revolutionary moment pass me by because of the opinions of others. My resignation led to Abba asking me to cancel my full traveling itinerary and get joined to my spiritual father.

I wish I could say this all happened in an instant, but there was sincere wrestling with God as I tried to cling to what was comfortable for me. I did not realize all the amazing lessons I was soon to learn. Had I known then what I know now, I would have made each transition much sooner! Hopefully, my story of this divine romance will accelerate your personal revolution to cast off the yoke of religion. Nevertheless, there I sat in South Carolina with no plan, only the invitation to recover the life of proximity to Jesus.

The very week I finally said yes to the complete undoing of my idea of ministry, a businessman called me: "Mark, I was praying for you, and the Lord wanted me to ask you what you needed." I jokingly replied, "I need a salary." Without hesitation, that man said, "That's why I called." He knew Yahweh was asking me to sit down and inherit a new set of blueprints, which I will share with you in the pages of this book.

That moment of complete surrender unlocked the provision of God that gave me three and a half years of intimacy to destroy the yoke of religion, get delivered from all inferior identities, and settle into the sweet spot of becoming a dearly loved son and bride. Yahweh had finally gotten me to a place where He could prove He loved me for me, not for what I could do for Him.

This book is my journey out of the busyness of Babylon and into the rest and peace of the Kingdom of God. I certainly do not have all the answers, but I want at least to share with you the blueprints I was able to receive in those formless moments in the wilderness of South Carolina. Those days of Abba's jealousy for me are the motivation for everything being shared within the pages of this book.

No matter your current vocation or background, may you find the grace to cast off the yoke of religion and all of its Babylonian tendencies and find yourself in a personal revolution of life. There is a new pace, untethered from time and the opinions of man, to hear a new sound of divine romance in what I call "the rhythm of the realm of rest."

Will you dare to answer the invitation to dance this dance with the Lover of your soul? Are you willing to get untethered from the sound of chaos and find a new pace for your life? Yeshua, the Prince of Peace, is calling you out of the chaos of your busyness and inviting you into a brand-new blueprint for your life. Will you take the leap to see what happens? I hope you do, because Abba has dreams that far exceed anything you could ask or imagine.

If you are looking for a quick fix, how to get to your dreams faster, or a lifehack to bring you greater productivity, this book is not for you. Transformation takes time, and anyone who would tell you different is selling you a lie. This is a book to encourage those who hunger for something real and know there is something more.

So, if you're tired and weary—

If you are feeling like there is a more excellent way to do life—

If you feel that our current standard of success is flawed—

Maybe you're finally ready to surrender to the way of Jesus.

Enjoy this book. I think it will give you some keys to assist in the new dance Jesus longs to teach you, a dance to the rhythm of the realm of rest.

CHAPTER ONE

Encountering the Shepherd-King

Now what? That was my question following the decision to cancel everything. For years, I had been busy traveling and preaching. I had no excuses for not diving deep into intimacy with Jesus now that my salary was covered, yet there I sat, twiddling my thumbs and trying to find something to do. In those early days, I struggled with what devotion actually looked like.

I took some time to read the Word but, to my annoyance, found that my mind was still looking for a sermon. I tried to pray, but if I sat still long enough, I would fall asleep. Religion wouldn't let me admit I was in need of rest. I had to be busy! So devotion became my morning routine, and then it was off to take on the next project for my family.

I certainly found ways to be productive around our home. I rearranged our entire backyard. I bought lawn equipment. I tackled every inch of overgrowth on my property to the very root. After weeks of relentless activity, sweat dripping from my brow, I began to realize:

ministry was not the enemy of devotion to Jesus. The enemy was my addiction to busyness.

We were finally settled into our home, and our backyard was completely cleared out just in time for the best season of all—fall! I knew there was only one project left: a firepit. When a few friends helped me to build a simple design, I did not realize how important this one project would be. This simple pit would become an altar in the fall of 2016, where a divine romance would begin with Jesus Himself.

My spiritual father, Damon Thompson, gave a divine instruction to our Kingdom family for those three fall months to sit alone and bathe ourselves in the Song of Solomon. I can remember thinking, "The Song of Solomon? A book of erotica. Even worse for a preacher who always had to preach something new every week, you are asking me to stay in eight chapters of the Bible for three months. Are you kidding me?"

Yet, what did I have to lose? Finally, I had sure direction from the Lord. I told myself I'd see how far we could stretch this out. Besides, this was a great excuse to be outside and break in the new firepit. Each morning, if weather permitted, I would start a fire and sit with my Bible, reading a book I had dismissed from the entirety of my spiritual journey with Jesus.

At the time, I never would have dreamed that I'd find my story within the pages of this obscure book—but I did. Little did I know that season of reading the Song of Solomon was only the beginning of my journey into God's rest.

The early church fathers called the Song of Songs a book of wisdom. You'll see this more clearly as we take this journey together. There are multiple ways one can interpret the Song of Songs. However, if you're only understanding it through the shallow lens of a sexual relationship between a husband and a wife, you'll miss the most important revelation of this song.

This song is, in fact, a clear representation of Christ and His bride. It's about the Shepherd-King casting out the fears and insecurities of an exhausted, dirty Shulamite who would become the bride by way of His perfect love. As a result, she overflows with the Bridegroom's love, becoming a feast for the nations. In the Song of Songs, we see Jesus, the Bridegroom-King, raising up His radiant Shulamite bride in the earth.

This book of divine romance is essential for the church today. It can reform the way we see evangelism, our purpose for gathering, and our daily lives. It's the story of how Jesus makes His bride beautiful and holy by casting out her fears with perfect love. Yahweh takes this overworked Shulamite, bound in fear, and restores her identity by His unfailing love.

God wants to raise you up, like the exhausted Shulamite, as His radiant bride, overflowing with your Lover's life, to become the feast for the nations and the wine to cheer others' hearts.

Walking with the Shepherd-King

Please don't stare in scorn because of my dark and sinful ways. My angry brothers quarreled with me and appointed

*me guardian of their ministry vineyards, yet I've not tended
my vineyard within.*
—**Song of Songs 1:6** *(TPT)*

It only took a few verses to find myself extremely uncomfortable, yet I also found my storyline hidden within
this peculiar song. Although I was not familiar with this
bridal language of the kisses and caresses of God, I could
identify with how the Shulamite saw herself and how she
had spent her time.

Her story was my story: overworked, exhausted, with
the complete loss of tenderness and zero confidence that
the Lord saw anything valuable in me. I had spent years
tending everyone else's vineyard (ministry) at the expense
of my vineyard within (identity). My gospel was fragile,
as I did not know life apart from the treadmill of performance. Who was I without a microphone and a pulpit?

This cry from the Shulamite describes nothing if not
modern-day ministry. We have perverted the process of
the believer by exalting ministry over the importance of
being rooted in identity. We take anyone gifted or with
any resemblance of a call of God upon their life and send
them to tend the collective vineyard without showing
them the importance of keeping their own. What is the result?

In the very next verse, the Shulamite asks, "Why
should I wander like a prostitute...?" (Song of Solomon
1:7). We take those Christ has chosen to be His very own
and turn their gaze to what they can do in the fields of
ministry. Could it be that in today's American version of
Christianity, ministry has become a prostitution ring?

The call to be the servant of all is not at the expense of our own hearts. We cannot allow another generation to believe their performance in ministry is more important than their intimacy with Jesus.

At twenty-two years old, I found myself on an international ministry platform. I was charismatic and wild, with a Pentecostal "gift" to communicate how disgusted God was with our sinful selves, among whom I was chief. However, it did not take long to realize our ministry had outgrown me. I was exhausted, dry, and no longer tender. The happy man my wife had married was now just a shell of a man, crumbling under the cares of the ministry. I was unable to receive the love of God because I was introduced to the ministry before I was truly introduced to Him.

Overwhelmed by the reality of the Shulamite's (our) story, there I sat, finally coming to grips with what Yahweh was truly doing in my life. He had delivered me from the machine of ministry to regain my tenderness in intimacy with Him. The time had come to inherit my true identity in Him instead of what the ministry machine thought I should be doing.

It all began to click. This was why I had to walk away from everything I knew. This was why Yahweh had asked me to cancel my itinerary. I had become the weary Shulamite, unsure of how He really felt about me. I don't know how long I sat by the fire that day, but Jesus was about to invade my life in a very personal way.

I remember closing my eyes, and to my surprise, I went into an encounter with the Good Shepherd. He was walking toward me with His hand held out to me, and He said,

"Come take a walk with Me." At that moment, I looked away to see my vineyard. It was overgrown, full of thorns, and absent of color. I looked back to Him while pointing at the obvious. To my surprise, He didn't change the invitation: "Come walk with Me."

With my hand in His, we walked together. I told Him about all the things we needed to fix so that my garden could be presentable. As the list unfolded, He interrupted me and said, "It's okay. Just walk with Me and let My Father handle your garden. He is an excellent vinedresser."

Every day after that, He came to walk with me. Eventually, I learned that the flaws of my vineyard were irrelevant. Yet each time we walked past, I started seeing fewer weeds and thorns. Things were beginning to bud and sprout. But I hadn't done a thing other than take a walk with the Good Shepherd!

Those walks were about convincing me of His love for me. I knew my days of wandering like a prostitute were over. This was where I would begin inheriting the mystical language of bridal identity. He loves me for me, not for what I do for Him.

Losing My First Argument with God

The argument I had with God at that point was not about fasting; it was about His love. These walks were extremely uncomfortable because He had one goal in mind: to shower me with affection. Do you know how extremely uncomfortable it is for a legalistic Pentecostal like me to receive the love of God without criticism?

Each time He would say over me who He thought I really was, I (like the Shulamite) met Him with another reason He should think twice about what He had just said. On one particular day, He interrupted my pity with a thundering statement: *"You will never talk Me out of loving you!"*

The tears flowed down my face like a waterfall. For hours, wave after wave of love came crashing into my world. I knew there was not a chance that I, or anyone else, would ever be able to win that argument with the Bridegroom-King! But it is our propensity to argue anyway.

You Are Lovely!

The Shulamite

Jerusalem maidens, in this twilight darkness I know I am so unworthy—so in need.

The Shepherd-King

Yet you are so lovely!

The Shulamite

I feel as dark and dry as the desert tents of the wandering nomads.

The Shepherd-King

Yet you are so lovely—like the fine linen tapestry hanging in the Holy Place.

—Song of Songs 1:5 (TPT)

Religion teaches us to talk like this. Unworthiness becomes a badge of honor, and we even argue with our Creator about our worth. We have conditioned ourselves to look within and see every flaw. If you grew up like I did, in a Pentecostal tradition, you might likewise have been conditioned by preachers who taught you to see the sin within. We were experts in the fall of man because we were convinced of God's displeasure over us as His failing creation.

Yet this is not the Jesus we meet in the Song of Songs. The Shepherd-King refuses to agree with our self-accusations.

Do you deny your Shepherd-King, too? Do you point back to your failure while He is showering you with affection? We need a revelation of the love of God, and that comes by way of surrendering our own idea of what this relationship is supposed to look like. This relationship with the Shepherd-King looks more like a bedchamber than a courtroom.

The Shulamite

Let him smother me with kisses—his Spirit-kiss divine. So kind are your caresses, I drink them in like the sweetest wine! Your presence releases a fragrance so pleasing—over and over poured out. For your lovely name is "Flowing Oil." No wonder the brides-to-be adore you. Draw me into your heart. We will run away together into the king's cloud-filled chamber.
—Song of Songs 1:2–4a (TPT)

There could be no truer statement than when A. W. Tozer said, "What comes into our minds when we think about God is the most important thing about us."[1] For years, religion has robbed us of this intimate knowledge of Jesus hidden within the Song of Songs. Because we have failed to see the intimate nature of the Godhead, we have missed the kiss that brought human nature into existence.

In those days sitting around the firepit, I learned that recovering the language of intimacy is vital because it restores our ability to receive our true identification as ones who are dearly loved.

Don't Miss the Kiss

The language in the Song of Songs may initially be uncomfortable for those who were not given permission in their journey with the Lord to experience the intimate language of God. But the ancient apostolic fathers, like Origen and Augustine, were no strangers to this mystic language. During the Middle Ages, St. Bernard of Clairvaux—who was a great Cistercian spiritual writer, noted preacher, and defender against heresy—authored eighty-six sermons from the book of Song of Solomon, fully developing the notion of spiritual marriage.[2]

You will quickly see that this language of intimacy has been available in your walk with God all along, but inheriting greater revelation may take someone giving you permission to see God in a new light. May this discussion grant you license for a new discovery of the nature of Jesus.

In the first chapter of the Song of Songs, the Shulamite begins to engage with the Bridegroom-King, and the first thing she cries out for is intimacy.

The Divine Kiss

"Let him smother me with kisses—his Spirit-kiss divine" (Song of Songs 1:2a TPT). This was the same kiss that breathed the divine life of the Deity into the dust of Adam when he became a living soul in the garden of Eden! The Shulamite's desire is face-to-face communion, in which His awakening breath fills her weary soul.

The truth is that all mankind, whether they realize it or not, are asking for the kiss of the Divine. This Spirit-kiss is a metaphor for intimacy with the Creator, where mud and Maker become one. You were born for this type of face-to-face communion with Jesus, and anything short of it is robbery of true devotion.

You may remember this Spirit-kiss from the moment when you first accepted Christ. You could not get enough of Jesus, and you wanted as much of Him as you could possibly have. Yet, because religion didn't equip you to cultivate your relationship with Jesus, the breath of that original kiss slowly dwindled.

His Caresses

The Shulamite goes on to say, "So kind are your caresses, I drink them in like the sweetest wine!" (Song of Songs 1:2b TPT). The caress is plural because the love of God is to be a continual experience. Anyone who has any history with God will tell you that there have been many times when the Lord has wrapped His loving arms around their lives to bring them to the present moment.

His caress began with His faithfulness to reach for you, even when you were not reaching for Him. Do you remember when He swooped into your darkness and transferred you into the kingdom of His marvelous light (Colossians 1:13)? He intervened and caressed you in His faithfulness. That was not to be a one-time experience: both the kiss and the caresses are designed to keep us through the storms of this life.

His caresses are His kindness toward us. I see these as the embracing love of God, which is so contrary to the God I was raised to know. I was raised to know God as one ready with lightning bolts to strike down filthy sinners. I find no futility in the caresses of God because He is constantly reaching to redeem, to restore, and to reveal His love for His people.

A Drink of Wine

In Brian Simmons's book *The Sacred Journey*, he reveals to us in elegant fashion the Hebrew wordplay between "kiss" and "take a drink (of wine)," being nearly the same word. He says, "The implication here is that God's lovers will be inebriated with His love, by the intoxicating kisses of His mouth."[3]

Have you ever experienced being in love? If you have, you know the feeling of not being able to get enough of the one you desire. You can't get off the phone without saying, "I love you," a million times. You're at work, but you're thinking about that special someone. Someone may say your name, but you can't hear through the noise of your daydream about the one you love.

The kisses and caresses are to be your daily drink of the intoxicating love of God. As awkward as it was to navigate those first few phrases of the Shulamite, they revealed a profound reality to my heart: I knew nothing about resting in the depths of His love. But there is a place of rest for the busy and overwhelmed heart, a place where He leads all His lovers. Would you allow Him to show you?

Learning to settle into a divine dance with God started when I read the Song of Solomon in front of the firepit every morning that fall. Since then, the revelation of being called to rest in God's love has only grown in my life.

WORKBOOK

Chapter One Questions

Question: Is your life characterized by unrelenting busyness? In what ways is the pace of your life keeping you from pursuing a divine romance with God?

_____

_____

_____

_____

_____

_____

_____

_____

_____

_____

_____

Question: When was a time you experienced the caresses and kisses of God? How can you posture yourself to experience that kind of intimacy with God continually?

_____

_____

_____

_____

_____

_____

_____

_____

_____

_____

_____

Action: *"You will never talk Me out of loving you!"* Spend some time quieting yourself in God's Presence. Let His voice overcome the negative voice trying to make you feel unworthy of His love. Allow Him to reveal to you that there's nothing you can do or say that will change His love for you.

Chapter One Notes

.

CHAPTER TWO

The Shepherd's Tent

The Shulamite to Her Friends

Please don't stare in scorn because of my dark and sinful ways. My angry brothers quarreled with me and appointed me guardian of their ministry vineyards, yet I've not tended my vineyard within. Won't you tell me, lover of my soul, where do you feed your flock? Where do you lead your beloved ones to rest in the heat of the day? Why should I be like a veiled woman as I wander among the flocks of your shepherds?

The Shepherd-King

Listen, my radiant one—if you ever lose sight of me, just follow in my footsteps where I lead my lovers. Come with your burdens and cares. Come to the place near the sanctuary of my shepherds.

—Song of Songs 1:6–8 *(TPT)*

In the midst of busyness, when this Shulamite was feeling dry and worthless, the one thing that saved her was her desire for more of her Beloved. It was not her faithfulness to keep her vineyard within; it was simply a desire that would not quit.

Her desire for more was not met with a scathing rebuke. The Bridegroom-King could have reprimanded her lack of care for her own vineyard. Instead, He offered her a resting place where her inner garden of tenderness could be restored.

Where is this place? It's the Shepherd's tent. In this generation, Yahweh is once again raising up the tent of David, a place of His Presence where those who feel unworthy, dark, and dry can find rest. This is a place of healing, not harshness. It's a place where you can find the pace of peace and where interior gardens can once again flourish.

This is the place where colorless Shulamites become radiant brides. It's a place absent the busyness of Babylon, so you can get rooted in a life of rest and peace. In this place, you will have to learn to sit still long enough for Abba to prune the areas of your life where you have overextended yourself.

Does such a place exist? Yes. Throughout church history, men and women who longed for more have untethered from the culture of their day to embrace a simpler life. These people admitted, like the Shulamite, that somewhere along the journey, they lost sight of Him, and they needed a place to reorient themselves to the gaze of the Lover of their souls.

You will not find this place because of your self-effort or discipline. This is the place where the Shepherd-King leads those who have a desire for more of Him.

A Place for Those Who Have Lost Sight of Him

The Shepherd's tent is a place of intimacy; however, it is also a corporate assignment. Yahweh has entrusted the local Kingdom family to become a place free of the idolatry of busyness. For too many years, the church has been infiltrated by the very culture of busyness we are called to reject, and therefore, we spend all of our energy projecting an image of ourselves instead of reflecting an image of our patient King.

How can we become a place of restoration for those who have been broken by the hustle culture if we are practicing the same thing in the name of church? People don't need a good service to attend once a week; they need an invitation into a lifestyle that will cause their lifeless garden to spring back to life.

Pastors and church leaders must begin to cultivate atmospheres of His Presence where people can find rest from their busy and distracted lives. Quit falling for the lie that people aren't spiritual. Rather, they are distracted by busyness and the cares of this life. We are not helping them by providing fast-paced, entertaining services where they can blow in and blow out, right back into their busy lives.

We must have places, Shepherd's tents, throughout the nations where the Holy Spirit is given free rein to paint the magnificent picture of Jesus for those who have lost sight of Him.

A Place to Receive Your Identity as Beloved

Second, the Shepherd's tent is the place where the Bridegroom-King leads His lovers (Song of Songs 1:8). Jesus has invited each of us into a covenant relationship where we are convinced of who we are because we have become fully convinced of how Jesus feels about us. For too long, religion has convinced us to identify with our dysfunction. However, Yahweh looks at this weary Shulamite and calls her His lover.

Once we are rooted in this reality, we become the initial witnesses to the transformative process of God's new creation order in this world. Abba, our Father, is asking you to become so whole, so convinced of Jesus' love, that you help to cultivate an atmosphere of rest, in which encounters with Him are the norm and not occasional interruptions of our busyness.

A Resting Place

Third, the Bridegroom-King call us to His tent as a resting place (Song of Songs 1:7). You will not find God in the busyness of this world. You must get rooted in a life of rest and peace because it's the only way truly to inherit the life of fruitfulness.

You must sit still long enough for Abba to prune the areas where you have overextended yourself. If you're in desperate need of rest, the Bridegroom-King doesn't hurry you into healing. He is not asking you to do a thing. Healing takes time, and so does establishing roots.

Saying yes to rest may be one of the most countercultural things you can do. Don't expect the angry brothers who are busy in their ministry vineyards to understand. They want you to snap out of this posture, much like Martha, who was upset at Mary for sitting at the feet of Jesus.

Please do not make the mistake of thinking that rest is laziness. Rest is a mighty tool in the process of growth and maturity. If we could understand that, we would not have to read the daily headlines of suicide, infidelity, and burnout in society today. This resting place will soon give way to strength as your budding garden begins to release the beautiful fragrance of Jesus to those around you.

A Place for Removing Burdens

Fourth, the Bridegroom-King calls us to His tent as a place that can handle our "burdens and cares" (Song of Songs 1:8 TPT). Again, the Shepherd's tent is more than just a dimension of intimacy. When you have been hurt, overworked, and not given the space to tend your vineyard within, you have the tendency to draw away from the people you need the most.

This tent is not just made up of spiritual dimensions. You need to be joined to a Kingdom family, the body of Christ. True rest doesn't come from isolation because experiencing Christ is two parts: experiencing intimacy with Christ and experiencing the fellowship of Christ by way of relationships with other believers. No one should shoulder their burdens alone. Remember, the Shepherd-King says that the Shepherd's tent is where He leads His lovers, plural. You need others for the journey.

The Shulamite testifies that His resting place "is anointed and flourishing" (Song of Songs 1:16 TPT). This is why He sends His weary to His tent: because the anointing within the family of God destroys yokes and lifts off heavy burdens.

What does the anointing do? Isaiah 10:27 says, "In that day the Lord will remove the heavy burden from your shoulders and break off the yoke of bondage from your necks because of the heavy anointing upon you!" (TPT). To what "day" or moment does this scripture refer? Isaiah 10:20 identifies it as the day when you no longer lean upon your abusers, but "lean fully on the faithfulness of the Lord Yahweh" (TPT).

Yahweh is saying, in effect, "I can send people there with burdens and cares because of the culture of rest you have established there. We are going to teach people how to get seated in beloved identity at a table called 'goodness.' Then they can begin to feast on the faithfulness of Jesus to the point where religious yokes and burdens can no longer stay attached to their lives."

First Peter 5:7 calls for everyone to give all their "worries and cares" to the Lord. That word "cares" refers to anxiety, being "drawn in different directions," or the distraction that causes anxiety.[4] In Jesus' Parable of the Sower, He calls these cares "the worries of this life" that crowd out the gospel message (Mark 4:19).

In Matthew 24:4–5, Jesus specifically warns against the misleading of false messiahs, which could also act as a worldly distraction to lead people astray. In Luke 11:46, He associates the burdens of the world with the "sorrow" that comes from a religious spirit, as embodied by the

Pharisees. Weighing yourself down with religious tasks leads to never feeling good enough.

God's anointing upon a church family manifests as sons and daughters of the King who are so nourished by the goodness of Jesus that it becomes impossible for the yokes of religion and busyness to burden them again. That's why the Bridegroom tells the Shulamite to "come with [her] burdens and cares" (Song of Songs 1:8 TPT). She is about to walk into an atmosphere so charged with the goodness of Abba that there is not a chance she can remain yoked to the anxiety of religious burdens!

If you and I are being made into witnesses of God's new creation in the world, we must begin feasting on the goodness that exists in His resting place—until we, too, are free from every religious yoke that weighs us down with anxiety and other burdens.

Your Journey to Freedom

Are you ready to become a front-row witness to God's transformative work? Do you want to be part of what God is doing to bring restoration to the burned-out and identity to the lost? Then start by embracing your own journey to get free. It's hard to establish a tent for the world-weary when you are still yoked to religion and the burdens of busyness.

You have to say yes to your new name, rooted in your identity as the beloved bride.

You have to say yes to a life of rest and peace.

You have to feast on His goodness until there's not a chance you'll ever be yoked to religion again.

But the sacrifices you make to free yourself, the things of the world you give up, will be more than worth it. A generation is in need of a safe place to exit Babylon—the system of religion and worldly busyness—so they can find their most authentic self. Yahweh set us free so that we could become His tent for others to find the eyes of the Bridegroom-King.

The problems you carry don't intimidate Him. Come with all of your burdens. Lay them aside and join Him. In the Shepherd's tent, you'll be protected from the elements.

Lord, raise up Your Shepherd's tent among the nations so that when we can't see You for ourselves and when we feel like we are all alone, we can come find rest in Your love, knowing You are crazy about us!

WORKBOOK

Chapter Two Questions

Question: Do you have an unquenchable desire within you for more of God? Why or why not?

_____

_____

_____

_____

_____

_____

_____

_____

_____

_____

_____

Question: What cares, worries, or burdens are keeping the gospel message from bringing you peace and rest? List them out and ask God to show you how to address these things so you can find a place of rest in Him.

_____

_____

_____

_____

_____

_____

_____

_____

_____

_____

Action: Embrace your own journey to get free from the yoke of religion. Spend some time in prayer, surrendering your heart to God so He can do this work in you.

Chapter Two Notes

_____

_____

_____

_____

_____

_____

_____

_____

_____

_____

_____

_____

_____

_____

_____

_____

_____

_____

_____

_____

_____

_____

CHAPTER THREE

Welcome to the World of Babylon

In the pages of carnal history there is no city more prestigious than Babylon. While you may imagine gold, jewels, and riches without measure, this city was actually located in an arid, flat desert, with no forests, mines, or rock to build with. Not to mention, the area did not have enough rainfall to raise crops.[5]

Through one of man's most incredible engineering accomplishments, people were able to divert the waters of the nearby Euphrates River by means of dams and enormous irrigation canals to create fertile soil and abundant agricultural growth unlike the world had ever seen—in a barren desert.

While Babylon was an incredible example of man's ability to accomplish great things, all of the resources used to support this massive city were man-made. That included their riches. While many who are absent from the knowledge of God would celebrate such an incredible human achievement, the Bible provides us with another perspective for viewing this vast human endeavor.

We first see mention of Babylon in chapter 11 of Genesis, when mankind decided to build a great city for themselves, "with a tower that reaches into the sky" (Genesis 11:4). In their hearts was a cry for fame and to gather all people to themselves. The tower of Babel represents human aspiration and pride and a spirit of boasting in human achievement. It is a pride that leads people to think they are godlike because of their material wealth.

Babylon represents the hustle culture of today that is believed to lead us to wealth and success. Men and women, young and old, do all that is within their power to achieve fame, independence, and self-sufficiency—all of which is celebrated in our post-modern society. Yet, what is heaven's perspective on such a place?

God calls Babylon "confusion." Confusion, simply put, is a place of uncertainty. If I were to take you today to the physical location of this human achievement, *you* would be confused, as this place of man-made wonder is deserted and has fallen into ruin. How could this be?

The Bible is very clear: when you, in the strength of man, try to build something in opposition to His original intent, it is destined for ruin.

Although Babylon the city no longer stands, its spirit lives on in the hearts of the ambitious sons of Adam. Without the knowledge of God's perspective on Babylon, we are destined to continue building our lives based upon the same faulty lens of humanism.

In the book of Revelation, chapter 18, a mighty angel steps out from the heavenly realm with great authority and shouts, "Fallen, fallen is Babylon the great! She has become a demonic dwelling place, a prison for every unclean spirit, unclean bird, and every unclean, detestable beast" (Revelation 18:2 TPT). This angel continues explaining to John the Beloved the real picture of such a luxurious man-made city. Although Babylon has caused all nations to drink the wine of her idolatry (money), growing their wealth "because of her power and luxury" (Revelation 18:3 TPT), her destruction is inevitable.

John then hears another voice: "My people, come out from her so that you don't participate in her sins and have no share with her in her plagues, because her sins are heaped as high as heaven and God has remembered her vileness" (Revelation 18:4–5 TPT).

God describes Babylon as a woman who has exalted herself and lived in luxury. He says that because of her power, she will experience grief and pain. With the American dream so ingrained in our hearts, we have the thorns and weeds of Babylon growing in our vineyard within, encouraging us to believe the same lies: if we could just get more exposure and amass more wealth, then all of our problems would be over. Yet God says that in just one hour, He will completely demolish this powerful system among the nations.

Why? Is God against us doing great things, having nice things, and filling ourselves with the finest of foods? No, but from my research, I believe Babylon's greatest sin in the eyes of God was that the cost of all this wealth was the trafficking of the bodies and souls of people. This antichrist system of power, money, and success became

God's enemy the moment His sons were reduced to slaves in order to create man-made success.

Today in America, there are people dressed in nice clothes, driving nice cars, and living in luxurious homes, with access to the finest healthcare and an abundance of food, but still enslaved. They are slaves to time, money, fame, and approval. This is where Yahweh draws the line and says, "Be free of her!" He did not create us to be slaves. We were intended to rule and reign as His bride from a place of intimacy and rest, not captivity and stress.

Awareness of this reality manifested acutely in my heart one morning in 2018, months before I moved to the Atlanta area. I woke up with a sense that the Holy Spirit wanted me to drive to Atlanta from South Carolina to make a simple declaration over the city. So I drove to one of my favorites places in the Atlanta area, the Battery, which is where all of the condos, restaurants, and shops are that surround the new Atlanta Braves baseball stadium.

I parked my car and walked to a large, open area while looking at the high-rise buildings downtown, and I said, "I call this city out of the busyness of Babylon and into the rest and pace of Covington, Georgia!" I then saw in the Spirit a pathway emerge from Atlanta to Covington, the city where we would one day establish The Shepherd's Tent. The Lord called it "the pathway of peace."

Weeks went by, and I finally came to Covington to spy out the land where we would soon live. There, in the corner of a coffee shop, I was facing a window and writing down the thoughts and dreams I believed Yahweh had given me for this city when two ladies sat down right behind me. My ears began to perk up when I realized I was overhearing an interview for an intern position in a certain city official's office.

As this short interview was coming to a close, the lady giving the interview made a couple of closing remarks to this soon-to-be intern. She said, "This town is beginning to experience a great influx of people from downtown Atlanta because people love the rest and pace that the city of Covington provides for its citizens."

It sounds bizarre, but I have learned that walking with God in moments of great obscurity leads to eventual powerful confirmations that you really are walking together. Just weeks after a simple declaration over the city, Yahweh had given me this powerful confirmation. I believe God *is* stirring people's hearts with a hunger for rest. People moving from the busyness of Atlanta into the slow-paced living of Covington further revealed that God is at work in this way. Together, we were creating a pathway of peace for those who have become slaves to the hustle culture of Babylon.

How Did We Become Slaves?

How does this Babylonian way of thinking enslave us today? The same way it placed Israel in captivity in 586 B.C., by taking a group of people who have forgotten the ways of God—which includes the Sabbath rest—and disconnecting them from their covenant identity to reidentify them by their work. Let me explain.

Babylon wants to reidentify you in order to enslave you to the idolatry of productivity. The goal is simple: if they can cause you to forget your God-given identity and get you to worship at the altar of work, they have successfully reduced you to slavery.

In chapter 1 of Daniel, King Nebuchadnezzar of Babylon gave instructions to his chief of staff, Ashpenaz, to bring him the young men of Judah. However, he only wanted the "strong, healthy, and good-looking young men" (Daniel 1:4). He wanted to "make sure they are well versed in every branch of learning, are gifted with knowledge ... and are suited to serve in the royal palace" (Daniel 1:4). Sound familiar?

Four young men were chosen: Daniel, Hananiah, Mishael, and Azariah. You may not recognize the last three names because, unfortunately, these three Hebrew boys have mostly been identified by their Babylonian names instead of their original, covenant names. You may know them as Shadrach, Meshach, and Abednego. But their true names are important for us to recognize since our society does not fully understand the significance of a person's name.

In the Hebrew culture, a name represented a person's identity and carried prophetic significance for his or her life. Look no further than the story of Abram to Abraham or Jacob to Israel. Name changes were a part of being in covenant with Yahweh.

Babylon understood the significance of names as well. In Daniel 1:7, Ashpenaz renamed these four Hebrew boys with Babylonian names. Notice the difference:[6]

- Daniel, meaning "God is my judge," was given the name Belteshazzar, which meant "lord of the straightened treasure."

- Hananiah, meaning "God has favored," was given the name Shadrach, which meant "the great scribe."

- Mishael, meaning "who is what God is," was given the name Meshach, which meant "guest of the king."

- Azariah, meaning "Jehovah has helped," was given the name Abednego, which meant "servant of Nebo."

It was not enough to change their diets and pump their brains with Babylonian indoctrination. The Babylonian rulers had to break these young men's identity from their covenant connection to Yahweh and reduce them to their work assignment within this system of slavery. Today, a similar world system works to disconnect you from your God-given identity so that you will bow to the altar of productivity. Babylon has successfully domesticated us, severing us from our true purpose, and now work defines who we are.

Don't believe me? Think about the first question you are often asked when meeting new people: "What do you do?"

This slavery actually begins much earlier than you may think, in the broken system we call public education. The day our children are introduced to "achievement motivation," the report card, is the day they learn to conform to the path of conventional wisdom and maintaining the status quo. We want our children to be good students; therefore, they must conform to the crowd and never challenge the system.

It's the American dream. Get good grades so that you can be accepted into a good college. Get into a good college program, and then you can get a good job—never once admitting that all you have become is a good slave. That way, you can eventually retire and enjoy the last ten years of your life.

I bet many of you reading this today have not thought deeply enough about the American nightmare we call success. We have been conditioned by Babylon to play it safe, following the conventional path to conventional success. But it's time to question this hustle culture that enslaves us to the clock and money. The slave-masters of Babylon are consciously—or for some, subconsciously—demanding you to produce. This system of slavery is greedy for more, striving daily to convince us that busyness is a virtue. Yet busyness is not a virtue; it is our vice.

Our obsession with hustle culture and climbing the ladder of success has caused us to become addicted to materialistic success, and we spend our lives striving to obtain it. This "work ethic" has conditioned society for generations. Now that we identify with our work, many people value their careers above the amazing responsibility of raising their children.

If you are on the ladder of success, take a moment to study the major figures who have inspired you to start the climb. These people who represent the elite of the

business world leave behind them a trail of bad relationships, divorces, and estrangement from their own
offspring. How could this culture of busyness be seen as
a virtue when it causes us to devalue those things that are
most important to Yahweh—like the family, mental
health, and a devotional life?

Are you aware of the reality of the culture we now live
in? People are murdering innocent children in their own
wombs to maintain their career path. We are sacrificing
our God-given responsibilities to get ahead. As if abortion
were not enough, Babylon has helped to fuel the fatherless
epidemic in our nation. The lies it has sold us about how
to get ahead in life have removed the head from many a
home.

Something has to change. People must break free from
the captivity of productivity in order for us to return to our
original intent. We must find the realm of rest.

Sleep for the Beloved

Once I'd finally cancelled my itinerary in early 2016, I
set my heart on spending more time in prayer and in the
Word. I would read several chapters of the Word and then
prepare my heart to pray, only to wake up an hour or two
later. I would feel so terrible because it seemed I had invited Jesus over for communion only to fall asleep in the
middle of the conversation.

After many days of this repeated pattern and much self-
condemnation for not being able to pray, the Lord made it
clear: "I didn't ask you to come off one treadmill to get on
another. It's time for rest."

Psalm 127:2 says, "In vain you rise early and stay up late, toiling for food to eat—for he grants sleep to those he loves" (NIV). The words "in vain" here are a translation of the Hebrew word *shav'*, meaning "uselessness, idolatry, evil."[7] In other words, burning the candle at both ends is useless, idolatrous, and evil. Denying yourself rest is actually a form of pride. However, Jesus gives the beloved ones sleep, and while they sleep, He provides for them.

Jesus, Our Blueprint

> Come to me. Get away with me and you'll recover your life. I'll show you how to take a real rest. Walk with me and work with me—watch how I do it. Learn the unforced rhythms of grace. I won't lay anything heavy or ill-fitting on you. Keep company with me and you'll learn to live freely and lightly.
> —*Matthew 11:28–30* (MSG)

Jesus had a lifestyle of rest despite all of the activity happening in His life. He modeled spiritual rest by being alone with His Father often, taking the early mornings for times of prayer (Mark 1:35). He even slept through storms (Matthew 8:24)! He also called His disciples away for times of rest (Mark 6:31–32).

Jesus is our blueprint for the life of rest. It's not that rest is merely a necessity or a luxury. It's an act of worship!

From Chaos to Rest

The earth was without form and void, and darkness was over the face of the deep. And the Spirit of God was hovering over the face of the waters.

—Genesis 1:2 *(ESV)*

The significance of the Hebrew word *shalom* is laid out so beautifully in Jefferson Bethke's latest book, *To Hell with the Hustle*,[8] that I want to share it with you here:

"The earth was without form and void" is a translation of the Hebrew word for chaos. Busyness has thrown many of our lives into chaos, and we spend most of our time trying to pick up the pieces before the next explosion. Even in all of this, we find the Holy Spirit hovering over our chaos, just as He did "in the beginning."

God's remedy for chaos is peace, or shalom. Each letter of the Hebrew word shalom is trying to tell us something:

Mem: water, chaos

Lamed: the staff, authority

Shin: teeth, destroy, consume

When we read these Hebrew letters from right to left, we can see that shalom means to have the teeth to destroy the authority of chaos. Rest is the strongest weapon you have to combat chaos. Even in Jerusalem's name we see this. It means, "you will see the mouth of peace destroy the authority of chaos."

We are all on a journey toward the New Jerusalem, this city of peace where chaos and busyness no longer have authority. God is calling you out of the chaos of busyness into the realm of rest! Will you answer the call?

WORKBOOK

Chapter Three Questions

Question: In what ways are you personally enslaved to time, money, fame, or approval? How does this impact your life and your relationship with God?

_____

_____

_____

_____

_____

_____

_____

_____

_____

_____

_____

Question: Does the idea of the American Dream appeal to you? Do you spend your life more committed to climbing the ladder of success than valuing the things God has called you to value (e.g. relationship with Him and others)?

_____

_____

_____

_____

_____

_____

_____

_____

_____

_____

_____

_____

Action: What is your dream? What is your definition of success? Spend time in God's Presence. Ask Him to show you *His* dream and *His* definition of success. How do your answers compare? What Bible verses support God's response?

Chapter Three Notes

CHAPTER FOUR

The Resting Place of His Love

There have been many books written in the past several years, especially in the area of self-help, that give us keys to reducing stress and learning to slow down. You can un-clutter your life and learn better time-management skills, but if you don't know where true rest comes from, you will still only know how to manage cycles of stress instead of truly finding a lifestyle of rest.

My goal is not to teach you how to manage stress. As my friend Bobby Lemley says, "We now live from vacation instead of for vacation." I want you to live in and from rest. Our rest is a person, and His name is Jesus. He is the promise given so that we may find what Hebrews 4:3 calls "the realm of confident rest" (TPT) in faith.

This is the promise for the people of God, and we are to do everything in our ability to embrace that promise and enter into it. Entering into rest should be as vital to us as receiving salvation. In the same way you left sin, you now are being called to leave busyness.

This book is not permission to do nothing; however, I believe it will grant you permission to do those things that actually matter. It's time to be, once and for all, set free from the restlessness of striving in your own will so you can find this realm of rest that is reserved just for you.

Consider Creation

Opposition to truth cannot be excused on the basis of ignorance, because from the creation of the world, the invisible qualities of God's nature have been made visible, such as his eternal power and transcendence. He has made his wonderful attributes easily perceived, for seeing the visible makes us understand the invisible. So then, this leaves everyone without excuse.

—Romans 1:20 *(TPT)*

Take a moment to look outside. Look at the grass, trees, and flowers. They aren't restless, nor are they wondering how they're going to grow leaves and sprouts. They have no need to freak out, because they are planted—better yet, rooted.

Creation preaches to us each day and in every season of the faithfulness of God. While the systems of this world are being shaken, the trees continue growing. While the things of this world are crumbling, the flowers keep blooming. Creation is at rest because it's connected to its source. In the same way, our source is the undeniable love of God, and when we are rooted in this reality, we are no longer subject to being shaken.

Rest Is Not Optional

As I have pondered this lifestyle of rest, I can't help but see the connection between rest and trust. I can personally attribute every anxiety in my life to an area where I have refused to trust the Lord and conform to His ways.

It was no different for the children of Israel. The writer of Hebrews 3 pointed out the mind of God toward Israel in their wilderness wanderings:

> *This ignited my anger with that generation and I said about them, "They wander in their hearts just like they do with their feet, and they refuse to learn my ways." My heart grieved over them so I decreed: "They will not enter into my rest!"*
>
> *—**Hebrews 3:10–11** (TPT)*

The people of Israel wandered in the desert because they refused to trust God and learn His ways. They did not just wander from a physical location. In their hearts, they wandered away from the realm of rest. How long will we also refuse to enter into His rest? Will we have to circle our same issues for forty years like Israel did in the wilderness? Do we refuse to learn a new way of life?

We have to stop looking at the ways of God as optional principles to be applied only when things start spiraling in a negative direction. Jesus announced Himself to His disciples as "the way and the truth and the life" (John 14:6 NIV). Just as we would agree that Jesus is truth, we must also see Him as the way of life.

May we once and for all be delivered from the notion that the Word of God is an intellectual ascent. It is a lifestyle to be lived!

A Place of Inconvenience

> *Today, when I speak, don't even think about turning a deaf ear to me like they did when they tested me at Meribah and Massah, the place where they argued with me, their Creator. Your ancestors challenged me over and over with their **complaining**, even though I had convinced them of my power and love. They still doubted my care for them.*
> *—Psalm 95:8–9 (TPT, emphasis added)*

In Hebrews 3 and 4, the writer was calling believers into the realm of resting in confident faith. The writer used the example of the children of Israel in the wilderness.

While many know of Israel's wanderings, many have not pondered the implications of their wanderings and how they could be seen in our own lives. Yet the propensities of our hearts are very similar to the fickleness of God's chosen people.

The real issue of restlessness within their own hearts was an issue of doubt and unbelief. Within days of being miraculously delivered from Egyptian bondage, Israel came to a moment of inconvenience. Instead of trusting the Lord to take care of them, they defaulted to the gateway of doubt: complaining.

Again, only days after watching Yahweh drown their enemies in the Red Sea, they found themselves complaining about a lack of water (Exodus 17). In a moment of inconvenience, they began to question God's power and love, specifically His care.

Our life in America is not that inconvenient. When we get sick, we can see a doctor. We don't have to hunt for food, because we have grocery stores. We have many blessings, like running water, central air, and dentists, just to name a few. However, when a moment like we experienced in 2020 comes to disrupt our way of life, it's amazing what is revealed from the human heart.

Like Israel, in moments of inconvenience, we want to blame our leaders and others for our problems instead of trusting that Yahweh is working (even in a pandemic) for our good.

Help Is on the Way

I think it is no accident that Yahweh would call His people into the realm of rest during a time of great inconvenience. These moments of inconvenience are not created by God, but they become opportunities to trust. Hebrews 4:3 says, "For those of us who believe, faith activates the promise and we experience the realm of confident rest!" (TPT).

As you are recovering from the impact of a pandemic, whether it was losing a precious loved one or your job, you may feel a million miles away from the promises Yahweh has given you. However, it's in moments like we are in right now that we can find this realm of rest if we trust His care.

It is your faith in Christ in the moments of inconvenience that activates the promise. So even when you don't know how God is working, you can trust that He is. This is not a time to be thinking about life before the inconvenience. That path only leads back to bondage. The Lord is using these difficult moments to bring you into a new realm.

I want you to know that the Lord is doing something in the midst of all this national turmoil for those who will trust in His care. Inconvenience is not a hindrance to the promises of God. Instead, it is the gate that leads you into the promise of the realm of rest.

Do You Trust in God's Care?

Those who live in the shelter of the Most High will find rest in the shadow of the Almighty.
—Psalm 91:1

In Psalm 91, we are called into a time of rest when it is seemingly impossible. We are called into the secret place of His love while being surrounded by terror, sickness, plagues, and thousands of deaths. How is this possible? By trusting in His care.

We see another example in Psalm 23:5 when the Good Shepherd sets up "a table before [us] in the presence of [our] enemies" (ESV). He offers us a feast of His goodness in the face of opposition.

Jesus is calling you into the primary revelation of this new way of life: resting and rooting yourself in His love. Ephesians 3:17 says, "Then, by constantly using your faith, the life of Christ will be released deep inside you, and the resting place of his love will become the very source and root of your life" (TPT). Your moments of difficulty are opportunities to use your faith!

Now we can look at a year like 2020 as a gift that brings us into a place of trust. We will be able to look back and see that all of the inconveniences activated the promises of God in our lives. Those days quarantined in our homes did not take us further from the promise. They were our entrance into the realm of rest that changed our lives forever.

All throughout the book of Psalms, David said, "I cried out to the Lord, and He cared for me" (Psalm 3:4; Psalm 37:17–18; Psalm 142:4–7). David faced many different obstacles, some external and some internal. Yet, in the midst of these issues, he called out to God, and God convinced David of His care. God will do the same for you!

It's time to get rooted in our Source. Like the trees, we may feel the wind, but our roots are deep, and we will continue to flourish in all that He has called us to be. It's time to ground ourselves, once and for all, in the reality of His perfect love toward us. These moments of inconvenience are bringing us into a measure of trust, activating His promises, and ultimately ushering us into the realm of rest.

WORKBOOK

Chapter Four Questions

Question: Do you think of finding rest as merely finding a way to manage your stress and busyness? Into what kind of rest is God *actually* inviting you?

_____

_____

_____

_____

_____

_____

_____

_____

_____

_____

_____

Question: Is your walk with God characterized more by trust or by complaining? When you experience difficult times, what do you tend to think about God and His involvement in your life?

_____

_____

_____

_____

_____

_____

_____

_____

_____

_____

_____

Action: *Jesus is calling you into the primary revelation of this new way of life: resting and rooting yourself in His love.* It's time to get rooted in your Source so that you can find peace and rest no matter what is happening around you. Spend some time asking God to reveal His trustworthiness to your heart.

Chapter Four Notes

CHAPTER FIVE

Abba Cares for You

When people get sick of the systems of Babylon calling them to bow constantly at the altar of productivity and they reach their breaking point, there needs to be a place where Yahweh can raise up a people that has said yes to cultivating a culture of rest.

People need a place to recover, a place that provides rest and calls them into complete trust in Abba's care. We need a place where we can regain confidence in His care and be free from the fear that drives us to produce a false sense of stability in material wealth. He gives us something the world doesn't have: His peace.

Yahweh is raising up His Shepherd's tent all over the nation as a place that will recover the Abba revelation. In His tent, people will inherit a theology that goes beyond knowing that Yahweh is powerful—He also cares.

Convinced of His Care

To enter the realm of rest, we have to become rooted in the reality of our identity as beloved. We have been given a promise from Jesus that the Father loves us with the very same love that He has for His perfect Son. As ones who are loved, we cannot let the reality of His care escape our hearts. If you believe you are loved by God, then you have to believe He cares. Jesus made it very clear:

> *You can buy two sparrows for only a copper coin, yet not even one sparrow falls from its nest without the knowledge of your Father. Aren't you worth much more to God than many sparrows? So don't worry. For your Father cares deeply about even the smallest detail of your life.*
> *—Matthew 10:29–31 (TPT)*

As we study the nature of God, we learn that He is omniscient (all-knowing), omnipresent (in all places at all times), and omnipotent (all-powerful), but that means nothing to us if we are not convinced that He cares deeply about the smallest details of our lives.

The entirety of Abba's nature is being leveraged in your life to work out every situation and scenario for your absolute good. His omniscience is used to order each step you take. His omnipotence is aimed at anything that would separate you from His love. His omnipresence is to ensure that you are never alone. All that Abba is displays His goodness to His creation!

True rest begins when we are so convinced of His love that we no longer question His care. You can be absolutely confident that He cares about whatever you're going through. He cares about your health, your finances, your family, your business, your friends, your city, your state, and your nation.

Understanding the Father's Nature

We are living in a moment when the Holy Spirit is helping the bride of Christ to inherit the most powerful revelation that Jesus carried: knowing Yahweh as Abba. If you grew up like I did, even your understanding of being filled with the Spirit was more about the power of God than the love of God. We focused on the manifestations of the Spirit seen in Acts 2 and failed to understand what actually happens within the heart of the believer. In Romans 8, Paul helps us, in this hour, to recapture what it really means to be filled with the Spirit:

> *The mature children of God are those who are moved by the impulses of the Holy Spirit. And you did not receive the "spirit of religious duty," leading you back into the fear of never being good enough. But you have received the "Spirit of full acceptance," enfolding you into the family of God. And you will never feel orphaned, for as he rises up within us, our spirits join him in saying the words of tender affection, "Beloved Father!" For the Holy Spirit makes God's fatherhood real to us as he whispers into our innermost being, "You are God's beloved child!"*
>
> *—Romans 8:14–16 (TPT)*

How can we know we have been filled with His Spirit? When we've heard the whisper from Abba: "You are My beloved son." In no way do I want to diminish the message of power and demonstration as it relates to the ministry of the Holy Spirit. However, I do believe a new standard is being raised for how people can know they have received the baptism of the Holy Ghost.

While many celebrate the fruit of the upper room encounter in Acts 2, they reject the root that must be established in the heart of one who has truly received. While I long to experience the fire, wind, and sound present within the experience, I'm thankful that Paul, in Romans 8, shows us what took root in their hearts.

The manifestations were only evidence that a people had just inherited the same declaration that Jesus received at His baptism: "This is my beloved Son" (Matthew 3:17 ESV). The question, then, must change if we want to restore this root of our identity as beloved. We cannot make speaking in tongues the only evidence. Instead, we must ask them if they inherited the personal whisper from the mouth of Abba claiming them forever as ones dearly loved.

Receiving this whisper will break off every chain of Babylonian influence as you begin to embrace a life of full acceptance into the family of God. That orphan spirit you once carried that caused you to labor and burn the candle at both ends for approval and accolades will be replaced with the ultimate approval of the One who formed and fashioned you in your mother's womb.

When you do receive His Spirit of fullness, two things will become irrefutable in your heart: Yahweh is your Father, and you are His beloved child! Those two primary revelations will break the spirit of religious duty off of your life. Then you will no longer live in fear of not measuring up.

A Theology of God's Care

Jesus called out with a loud voice, "Father, into your hands I commit my spirit." When he had said this, he breathed his last.
—**Luke 23:46** *(NIV)*

Last words are everything. Some of the most quotable words came from the wisdom of men and women who were coming to the end of their lives. These words above were spoken as the very last statement Jesus would make on that Good Friday, hanging naked from the tree of crucifixion. His were no ordinary words; they were a profound statement of confidence in knowing He had a Father who cares.

In an hour of incredible pain, how could Jesus muster up the strength to make such a statement? What measure of trust in the nature of Abba's care must be present at the moment one stares into the face of death?

Jesus was quoting Psalm 31:5 when He said, "I entrust my spirit into your hands." Psalm 31 could be summed up as a psalm of trust in the God who cares. Take a moment and read it for yourself. The psalm goes on to say, in verse

24, "So cheer up! Take courage, all you who love him. Wait for him to break through for you, all who trust in him!" (TPT).

And so, those who watched Jesus' cruel death heard from His lips a quote from a psalm calling on total trust in the care of Abba. There upon the cross, in the midst of pain and great affliction, He found rest in the care of His Father.

It seems possible that this theology of the care of God is a path to accessing new life—the resurrection life, a whole new way of living. In reading this book, are you struggling to lay down the old way of doing things? Sometimes we hold on to things because we are not convinced that He cares enough to give us something better. Maybe we hold on to the path of conventional wisdom because we are not convinced that He will provide for us on the unconventional path of hearing and obeying His word.

Simply consider how much Abba cares for you. As you come to understand this truth more fully, your struggle will melt like wax. The greatest revelation we can receive is that learning to rest in Abba's care is our access to abundant life. Take a moment and meditate on these passages from the book of Psalms:

- Abba cares for us from the moment we take our first breath (Psalm 139:16–18).

- In your trouble, God cares for you (Psalm 31:7–8).

- Not even a mouse can escape His care (Psalm 36:6 TPT).

- His care is faithful (Psalm 37:28).

- God's care leads us into peace (Psalm 37:29 TPT).

- His care is constant (Psalm 57:3 TPT).

- You can see His care everywhere (Psalm 119:64 TPT). Birds don't even plan their meals, and God provides for them (Matthew 6:26).

- You think Marvel superheroes are awesome? God is our hero! He Himself is untouchable, and He acts as our protector (Psalm 145:20).

Look throughout the entire ministry of Jesus. He is constantly referencing the care of His Father for all of us. Even in the smallest details, no matter how insignificant you may think they are, God cares (Matthew 10:29–31).

As we saw in the last chapter, an entire generation of the children of Israel was locked out of the Promised Land because they failed to believe in Abba's care. Only two men believed, Joshua and Caleb, and they went on to experience their promise of rest. Everyone else did not because they could not. They failed to enter the Promised Land because they failed to trust that God would care for them in every circumstance.

So whatever you are doing and no matter where you are in this journey of life, you get an invitation into the realm of rest. Why don't we take a moment right now to enter into rest? We can follow this simple path directly into the Presence of God. All you have to do is "pour out all your worries and stress upon him and leave them there, for he always tenderly cares for you" (1 Peter 5:7 TPT).

May this become the beginning of you recapturing the theology of Abba's care. May today be the day you enter into the realm of rest. Learn to leave your burdens and cares where they belong—at the feet of the One who truly cares for you!

WORKBOOK

Chapter Five Questions

Question: What is your view of God? How do you believe He views you? How does this affect your ability to trust Him and enter into rest? What do you think is the root of your struggle to lay down the old way of doing things?

_____

_____

_____

_____

_____

_____

_____

_____

Question: What do you think it means to be filled with the Holy Spirit? What do you think is the evidence of being filled with the Spirit? How does Romans 8:14–16 say that we can know we have been filled with the Holy Spirit?

_____

_____

_____

_____

_____

_____

_____

_____

_____

_____

Action: Take a moment right now to enter into rest. Follow this simple path directly into the Presence of God. All you have to do is "pour out all your worries and stress upon him and leave them there, for he always tenderly cares for you" (1 Peter 5:7 TPT).

Chapter Five Notes

CHAPTER SIX

The Restlessness of a Fickle Heart

But Jesus did not yet entrust himself to them, because he knew how fickle human hearts can be. He needed no one to tell him about human nature, for he fully understood what man was capable of doing.

—John 2:24–25 *(TPT)*

One morning, as I was reading the Scriptures, this passage that I have read so many times before hit my heart in a deep way. After a few moments of meditating on why this verse had pierced me so deeply, I heard the inner whisper of the Holy Spirit ask, *"What part of the Kingdom of God has not been entrusted to you because of the fickleness of your heart?"*

We are being rescued out of the busyness of Babylon to find a new rhythm in the realm of rest. It's what we are crying out for. It's something we should earnestly seek in the Lord. However, if we truly seek to live in rest, we cannot see rest through the fickle lens of temporary relief from challenging times. Rather, true rest is the way of Jesus and a lifestyle to embrace.

The Scriptures are clear concerning how we should ask God for something. James, the brother of Jesus, said, "Just make sure you ask empowered by confident faith without doubting that you will receive. For the ambivalent person believes one minute and doubts the next. Being undecided makes you become like the rough seas driven and tossed by the wind. You're up one minute and tossed down the next. When you are half-hearted and wavering it leaves you unstable. Can you really expect to receive anything from the Lord when you're in that condition?" (James 1:6–8 TPT).

This wavering in our hearts will keep us out of sync with the Master and prevent us from entering true rest. We can see this within the life of the disciples in two familiar Gospel passages. In Mark 4:37–38, Jesus was asleep in the boat while the disciples were shouting for their lives as the ship was tossed by a tumultuous storm. In Matthew 26:36–46, Jesus was awake, praying in the hour of great tribulation, yet the disciples were asleep.

These two passages reveal a great truth about the human heart. Without being rooted in the rhythm of rest in God, we find ourselves awake to what Jesus sleeps through and asleep through what Jesus asks us to be awake to. In Mark 4, the disciples did not rest in the fact that Jesus said they would go to the other side. Yet in Matthew 26, the disciples slept through the very hour when the Master needed them awake.

The Lord wants to entrust us with His life of rest. However, He will not rest upon the restlessness of our fickle hearts.

The Fickle Heart

The issue in John 2 was that although more and more people began to give their allegiance to Jesus, their allegiance was directly connected to His ability to perform miracles (John 2:23). Jesus would not entrust Himself to these people because He knew their hearts were fickle (John 2:24). If their motivation to follow Him was based on what He could do instead of who He was, He knew their allegiance would remain unstable.

The word *fickle* means to be "marked by lack of steadfastness, constancy, or stability."[9] Someone who is fickle is "given to erratic changeableness,"[10] especially as it relates to "one's loyalties, interests, or affection."[11] No wonder Jesus would not entrust Himself to those people! He knew it would be incredibly exhausting for them to follow Him for the wrong reasons.

Some followed Him for the miracles, but you find another group of people who followed Him because they were fed by Him. Jesus did not come into the world so that the world could be wholly dependent upon His actions. He came to model for the world a way of life that is completely yielded to the Father. That way of life is to become our permission to access the same relationship He shared with His Father and experience the same results. Hear the words of Jesus:

Why would you strive for food that is perishable and not be passionate to seek the food of eternal life, which never spoils? I, the Son of Man, am ready to give you what matters most, for God the Father has destined me for this purpose.
—John 6:27 (TPT)

Many people today are still trapped in the lie that Jesus came to form a religion of works and rules that would lead to the acts of God. This works-based righteousness puts us on the exhausting treadmill of performance, constantly working for the hand of God, when we could find rest in His finished work on the cross. This is where you discover you already have the heart of God. Would you not receive from the hand of God if you knew you already had His heart?

So, what is the answer for this fickle heart? It's a personal encounter with the steadfast love of God. On the cross, Jesus laid you a path to an intimate relationship with your loving God.

God's Steadfast Love

Many people think God is given to sudden and unaccountable changes of mood and behavior because we are, but I can promise you that He is nothing like us.

For my thoughts about mercy are not like your thoughts, and my ways are different from yours. As high as the heavens are above the earth, so my ways and my thoughts are higher than yours.
—Isaiah 55:8–9 (TPT)

We are created in His image, and by way of the Holy Spirit, we are being renewed to God's original intent for us. There is nothing fickle in Abba. He will not change His mind about you. How could the God who does not change—who "is the same yesterday, today, and forever" (Hebrews 13:8)—be given to sudden shifts depending on the behavior of broken human beings? Our illiteracy regarding God is a source of our restlessness.

Why do so many pastors and church leaders burn out and so many Christians find themselves exhausted in seeking the Lord? It is because we are constantly seeking the approval of a god made in our image. We must be delivered from the "pull yourself up by the bootstraps" religion because the moment you say, "*I* will do this," you have exchanged grace for the law. We can no longer submit to the heavy burdens of the Pharisees. We must confess what the Pharisees could not: we can't fix our fickle hearts.

You will never free yourself from busyness and fickleness by exerting your own will. Heini Arnold wrote that "as long as we think we can save ourselves by our own will power, we will only make the evil in us stronger than ever."[12] Why don't we just surrender now to a new way of life instead of strengthening our bonds of religion by our own effort?

I am committed to completely rejecting the legalistic image of God that the Pharisees promoted. I am yielding instead to the image I see written in the love story that Christianity-as-religion did not want me to read. Lamentations 3:22–23 says, "The faithful love of the LORD never ends! His mercies never cease. Great is his faithfulness;

his mercies begin afresh each morning." Psalm 89:1 says, "This forever-song I sing of the gentle love of God! Young and old alike will hear about your faithful, steadfast love—never failing!" (TPT).

These are the realities on which we stand in Christ! We stand on His faithfulness and not our own. The Father will not change His mind about us, because He will not change His mind about Jesus. The Father, the Son, and the Spirit have unwavering affections toward us.

Running After You

One day, Jesus warned His disciples of His coming crucifixion. Peter interrupted Jesus, saying, "Even if I have to die with you, I will never deny you!" (Matthew 26:35). In the hour of temptation, the "I will" turned into a complete denial of Jesus. However, one disciple remained at the feet of Jesus, even to the cross: John the Beloved.

John called himself "the disciple Jesus loved" (John 13:23). It wasn't the one who boasted in his own will who made it through the hour of temptation; it was the one who knew the steadfast love of Jesus.

Jesus' unwavering love is what heals devotional inconsistency. You didn't make it this far because you were disciplined or because of your knowledge. You only made it this far because Jesus has remained faithful to you. When you were fickle, He was steadfast (2 Timothy 2:13). When you were prayerless, He never stopped interceding on your behalf before the Father.

Seeing Him as steadfast is how we exit the fickle pursuit of things and enter into the rest of a steadfast devotion to Jesus. It's the only path out of the restlessness of a fickle heart and into the grace of Abba. We must stop making God in our own image. Just ask the prodigal son— the Father doesn't make you do the walk of shame. He comes running toward you!

Now to ask you a question: What part of the Kingdom of God has not been entrusted to you because of the fickleness of your heart? This has an answer. Because allegiance is not based on performance or the pursuit of things, "[t]hose who walk along his paths with integrity will never lack one thing they need, for he provides it all!" (Psalm 84:11 TPT).

Rest is His path. As the Good Shepherd, "He offers a resting place for me in his luxurious love. His tracks take me to an oasis of peace near the quiet brook of bliss. That's where he restores and revives my life" (Psalm 23:2–3a TPT).

The Spirit of Adoption

May God move your heart to the most authentic baptism into His steadfast love. After all, "you have received the Spirit of adoption as sons, by whom we cry, 'Abba! Father!'" (Romans 8:15 ESV).

It is the gift of the Holy Spirit and our yielding to the revelation of the gospel that grant us the healing of the fickle heart and the grace for a steadfast commitment to a life of devotion to Jesus. Devotion to Jesus will not come because you have found a great Bible-reading program with all the steps laid out for you. The grace for stead-fast devotion to Jesus is birthed out of the reality that there's nothing you can do to talk God out of loving you extravagantly. Once you embrace this truth, you will no longer ascend the mountain of devotion in your own might. Rather, you will be carried like a bride across the threshold of her new home.

Life in the Spirit is much more than speaking in tongues. It's about knowing you are dearly loved by Abba and He doesn't change His thoughts about you. This is the beginning of true rest! Paul prayed this very reality over the church in Ephesus when he prayed that "the resting place of his love [would] become the very source and root of [their] life" (Ephesians 3:17 TPT).

There is no rest in chasing miracles or perishable, carnal items. There is only rest in knowing the Father loves you with the same love He has for His Son! You now share in that inheritance. No more proving your-self, only receiving your true self. No need to dive into the depths of your former nature. Simply dive into the divine nature, which is filled with the steadfast love of Abba. Let's continue this journey together into the realm of rest.

WORKBOOK

Chapter Six Questions

Question: What part of the Kingdom of God has not been entrusted to you because of the fickleness of your heart? Is your motivation to follow Jesus based on what He can do instead of who He is? Does that affect the steadiness of your walk with Him? Why or why not?

_____

_____

_____

_____

_____

_____

_____

_____

_____

_____

Question: What do you think it means to surrender to a new way of life instead of strengthening your bond of religion by your own effort? What do you think it looks like to surrender to a lifestyle of rest?

_____

_____

_____

_____

_____

_____

_____

_____

_____

Action: Come before God and confess that you can't fix your fickle heart. Confess that you are done trying to prove yourself and are ready to receive your true self. Allow God to pour His unchanging, unshakable love into your heart.

Chapter Six Notes

CHAPTER SEVEN

Learning to Rest in a Time of Chaos

For during the time of Noah God patiently waited while the ark was being prepared, but only a few were brought safely through the floodwaters: a total of eight souls.
—1 Peter 3:20b (TPT)

Do you recall what the Bible says about the days of Noah? Noah was living in a day when an odd paradox existed. People were eating and drinking merrily (Matthew 24:38), yet the earth was filled with violence and injustice (Genesis 6:11). No, I am not talking about 2020, although the days are oddly similar. In Noah's day, humanity had become wicked to the point that all they thought about was doing evil.

During a time when humanity was completely wicked, God had a plan. In the midst of such horrid conditions, Yahweh called a man named "Rest" and gave him the blueprints that would save the world.

Grace in the Eyes of the Lord

A man named Noah, which in Hebrew means "rest,"[13] was able to lift his eyes above the chaos of his day to find grace in the eyes of Yahweh. Many know this story very well yet miss its most important truth: this is not a story about Noah, but about what Noah found in the eyes of the Lord.

Noah had discovered a place of intimate rest in a time of chaos, and this gave him the ability to see something no one else could see. In a time of great evil and impending judgment, Noah found grace. He was able to look above what was going on in the culture and focus on God.

That place of intimate rest birthed the blueprints to save the human race. Although Noah was considered a man of integrity, his righteousness had nothing to do with his behavior. Noah's obedience to build something no one had seen (an enormous boat) for something no one had ever heard of (a cataclysmic deluge of rain) was made possible by finding grace in the eyes of the Lord.

We must get delivered from the religious standards of narcissism that keep us navel-gazing—preoccupied with our faults and failures. It's past time we quit disqualifying ourselves from the empowering grace Yahweh longs to give His people! Moreover, we must stop living in reaction to current events that distract us from the real work required to effect change in the world. It's time to take our eyes off of our natural circumstances.

Loyal Followers

God had a plan in the days of Noah, and He is moving in this moment as well. Yahweh is not sitting on His throne with sweat on His brow. Although many ministers are trumpeting fear-based messages of urgency, He is not calling us to gather urgently in reaction to our current circumstances. The Lord is looking for something entirely different. He is not looking for a heart of reaction, but one that is loyal to Him: "For the eyes of the LORD run to and fro throughout the whole earth, to give strong support to those whose heart is blameless toward him" (2 Chronicles 16:9 ESV).

God is looking for loyal followers, not reactionary ones. The Father is calling us back to the blueprint of Jesus. Jesus was not found running in reaction to the chaos of His day or being pulled into the urgency of the hour. If that were true, Lazarus would never have been dead for four days, Jesus would not have slept through storms, and He would have selected more disciples.

Jesus didn't offer His disciples a seminar on hot-button cultural issues. Instead, He gave them permission to share in the same intimacy He had with the Father. He taught them about His Kingdom, which was the true education needed to bring cultural transformation. He wanted His disciples to know how to trust in the Father and rest in His care, no matter the circumstances they were facing.

What are you going to do when you're confronted with the chaos of this bleeding culture? God is seeking someone who is at rest, not consumed with the headlines or trending causes of the day. He is looking for someone who can lift their eyes to His and take comfort in His grace!

There is grace available to all the sons and daughters of God. It's a grace to see redemption in every story and to see heaven invade a time of evil. That way, we can build with His blueprints instead of being distracted by man's reactionary attempts to fix the culture.

May we receive the grace to turn off the noise of culture, turn our eyes from the latest "breaking news" headline, disconnect from big tech, and find the realm of rest. That's where we can see what the Father is doing. In His eyes, we can see what He wants established on the earth. From that place, we can build with confidence according to the blueprints that liberate all humanity from the power and dominion of sin and chaos.

Blueprints for the Ark

> By faith Noah, being warned by God concerning events as yet unseen, in reverent fear constructed an ark for the saving of his household. By this he condemned the world and became an heir of the righteousness that comes by faith.
> **—Hebrews 11:7** *(ESV)*

The man of rest, Noah, was given specific instructions from Yahweh to build the ark. I believe we are receiving blueprints for an ark in our day as well so that we can show a generation how to navigate the troubled flood waters it's experiencing. Yahweh calls us out of our humanistic attempts to liberate a world in bondage to restlessness and the tyranny of the urgent to inherit the only answer for the world: Jesus!

Jesus is the blueprint we are to follow to become the solution to the world's problems. However, you can't become a solution to the world's problems while still being enslaved to its system of doing things. Just look at Facebook or Twitter. We see plenty who are quick to tell us what they are for or against, but who is following the blueprint of Christ? Jesus said, "If anyone would come after me, let him deny himself and take up his cross daily and follow me" (Luke 9:23 ESV). We must make this decision: Will we represent the King and His Kingdom, or will we continue the chaotic cycle of restlessness?

Yes, I know the world is operating in lawlessness, deceived by false narratives and conspiracy theories. But our answer is to rise up like Noah did, content to build according to his God-given blueprint for the sake of rescuing his family. You don't need to spend your days pointing out the problems. Noah's obedience was found in building what God asked of him, not pointing fingers at those in rebellion. Scripture never records a sermon preached by Noah, yet his obedience caused him to be identified as a preacher of righteousness. Noah's life of obedience was the message. His life screamed the Kingdom of God!

Jesus, too, shows us the way by letting His life be the message. As a white man living in a day when racial tension has become fever-pitched, I cannot be satisfied just to grab a sign, attend an event, post on social media, and check the box to show the world I am not racist. My answer for racial injustice is to build, according to God's blueprint, a place where every African American son and daughter of the Lord can find a home among our Kingdom family.

We aren't ignoring the issues. From rest, Yahweh sends us to establish the answer for any problem our world faces. Every day, we continue to build a revival culture here in Covington, Georgia. With each meal, time of prayer, and teaching, we are condemning the rebellious actions of our generation. We refuse to get distracted by the roller coaster of the daily news cycle, because we are working daily in Jesus to build the solution to the problem.

Remember that Jesus is the blueprint we are called to follow! Just as Noah built according to God's specific plan, we build with Abba's blueprint for rest. In this way, our families can abide safely and securely when surrounded by troubled waters. May we be a people who forsake anxiety, fear, and urgency to find grace and rest in God's eyes in a time of turmoil.

WORKBOOK

Chapter Seven Questions

Question: Are your eyes so focused on your own weaknesses and inadequacies or on the current events in society that you cannot hear the leading of the Holy Spirit in your life?

_____

_____

_____

_____

_____

_____

_____

_____

_____

_____

Question: Is your life a message that points to God's blueprint for living? If not, what needs to change?

_____

_____

_____

_____

_____

_____

_____

_____

_____

_____

Action: You have a decision to make. Allow the Holy Spirit to stir your heart. Will you continue the chaotic cycle of restlessness, or will you represent the King and His Kingdom?

Chapter Seven Notes

CONCLUSION

A Divine Pause

In 2015, when the Lord first spoke to me about the spirit of 1776 coming upon this generation, I did not realize how important that word would become in 2020. But now it seems that the revolution is upon us. The world is groaning for the children of God to be present and demonstrate a better way. This is not a revolution that will come by way of war or might. It is a countercultural revolution of rest.

God calls us to rest in times of great restlessness. In 2020, during the time of the writing of this book, we faced the coronavirus pandemic, which brought us into a moment of forced rest (social distancing), or what I like to call a divine pause. While this has brought about many challenges, the Lord was orchestrating it all for our good.

We, as the sons and daughters of God, are being called into a seat of peace, to ascend the mountain of devotion and receive a new pace for life. The 2020 pandemic was unexpected, but I believe it became an access point for the realm of rest.

Many years ago, Bob Jones released a prophecy concerning a hundred-year timeframe, showing him what God planned to do through each decade. This is the portion of prophecy concerning the 2020s:[14]

> *The 2020s will reveal the rest of God. To where the body will come into a place of resting in God, where God will rest in us. And in this rest, the enemy will not be able to do warfare because we are resting in God and He is resting in us, and He will accomplish the things He means to do in a people that is at rest. He has always wanted a people that will come into His rest. There never has been one but rest is on the way.*

The divine pause has begun, but will you allow this to be just a moment in time, or will you allow it to become a brand-new blueprint for your life? Abba wants to prepare us for a whole new world and way of life, one centered on the Presence of Jesus.

No Return to Normal

In 2020, the systems of man were shaken, forcing us to rest and look for a new way to do life. However, we are not called to return to "normal." Instead, we are being called into something greater!

To those who have bowed before the altar of productivity, rest feels like captivity. However, the people of the Kingdom can know that God's divine pauses strategically place us in an incubator for the creation of a new world called "heaven on earth." God's wisdom can come to invade our rest with the creation of this new world.

We are being called to slow down and inherit the wisdom for a new way of living. This divine pause can become the blank canvas on which the creative force of wisdom paints a new blueprint for life—your life, personally, and the lives of those around you. This is a time of great invitation for proximity and alignment to the way of Jesus, for musing in the garden of Yahweh's delight. It's a time to cultivate intimacy with the Bridegroom-King and partner with our Beloved in the ministry of intercession.

Let's say yes to becoming the manifestation of the realm of rest—inheriting blueprints for a new day and helping to bring about the creation of a new world!

REFERENCES

Notes

1. Tozer, A. W. *The Knowledge of the Holy.* Harper, 1961.

2. Gill, Katherine. "Bernard of Clairvaux." In Deeana Klepper, Gender in Medieval Christian Mysticism. Boston University, 2010. http://people.bu.edu/dklepper/RN413/bernard_sermons.html.

3. Simmons, Brian. *The Sacred Journey: God's Relentless Pursuit of Our Affection.* Broadstreet Publishing Group, 2015.

4. *Blue Letter Bible*, "Strong's G3308 – merimna." https://www.blueletterbible.org/lang/lexicon/lexicon.cfm?Strongs=G3308&t=NIV.

5. Clason, George Samuel. *The Richest Man in Babylon.* Penguin, 1926.

6. *Blue Letter Bible*, "Dan 1:7." https://www.blueletterbible.org/nlt/dan/1/1/t_conc_851007.

7. *Blue Letter Bible*, "Strong's H7723 – shav'." https://www.

blueletterbible.org/lang/lexicon/lexicon.cfm?Strongs=H7723 &t=KJV.

8. Bethke, Jefferson. *To Hell with the Hustle: Reclaiming Your Life in an Overworked, Overspent, and Overconnected World.* Thomas Nelson, 2019.

9. *Merriam-Webster Dictionary*, "fickle." https://www.merria m-webster.com/dictionary/fickle.

10. *Merriam-Webster Dictionary*, "fickle."

11. *Lexico*, "fickle." https://www.lexico.com/definition/fickle.

12. Arnold, Johann Heinrich. *Freedom from Sinful Thoughts.* 1974. 2nd edition. Plough Publishing, 2014, p. 82.

13. *Blue Letter Bible*, "Strong's H5146 – nōaḥ." https://www. blueletterbible.org/lang/lexicon/lexicon.cfm?Strongs=H5146 &t=KJV.

14. Joshua Michael Ballard. "Bob Jones 100-Year Prophecy (Audio)." Recorded February 22, 2011, Bethel Supernatural School of Ministry, Bethel Church, Redding, CA. YouTube video. May 27, 2019. https://www.youtube.com/watch? v=xXZ22oVNk2I.

About the Author

Mark Casto lives in Covington, Georgia, with his wife, Destani, and their four children, Elijah, Ezekiel, Elliana, and Eden. He is the pastor of The Shepherd's Tent in Covington, where they are hosting the Presence of God and creating a safe place for artists, entrepreneurs, and those burned-out from the system of religion to find rest in the Presence of Jesus.

If you would like to connect with Mark Casto, visit www.theshepherdstent.com or email him at mark@theshepherdstent.com.

Made in the USA
Monee, IL
16 June 2023

35956741R00063